Forty is the New F Word

WENDY SMITH

Forty is the New F-Word
© 2024 Wendy Smith

All rights reserved. No part of this publication may be reproduced, distributed, or transmitted in any form or by any means, including photocopying, recording, or other electronic or mechanical methods, without the prior written permission of the publisher, except in the case of brief quotations embodied in critical reviews and certain other noncommercial uses permitted by copyright law.

ISBN - 979-8-35097-500-0
eBook ISBN 979-8-35097-501-7

Table of Contents

1. Fear 1
2. Family 4
3. Friendship 7
4. Forgiveness 10
5. Function 13
6. Fatigue 16
7. Fitness 20
8. Failure 25
9. Fierce 28
10. Fashion 31
11. Feeling Good 34
12. Foxy 37
13. Fulfilling 41
14. Free 46

CHAPTER 1

Fear

An unpleasant often strong emotion caused by anticipation or awareness of danger; reason for alarm
To be afraid of; to have reverential awe of[1]

I CAN HEAR IT NOW: "WHY IN THE WORLD DID SHE choose to begin with fear?" To be transparent, it's because that was the first "F" word I associated with turning 40. I was filled with so much dread over that major birthday milestone. If you can honestly answer that you looked forward to that birthday, keep reading (maybe skip this chapter, but keep going). I promise it will get better! If you were like me and associated turning 40 with things like "middle-aged," "I'm officially getting old," or "what is happening to my body," this chapter is for you.

I'm not usually a diva. In fact, I am about as far away from diva as you can get. I am, however, a people person and I love a good party. To make this birthday more palatable, I demanded a party to celebrate this occasion. I understand we've just met, but you need to know that I am not the type of person to "demand" things. I don't think I've ever demanded anything in my life until this party, but if I was going to turn 40, it would be with a bang! My poor hubby. He is not a party person or really a people person, yet

---

[1] Merriam-Webster. (n.d.). Fear. In *Merriam-Webster.com dictionary*. Retrieved August 23, 2024, from https://www.merriam-webster.com/dictionary/fear

he was tasked with the planning. Y'all, I invited about 100 people to the backyard BBQ, and it was a BIG night. All of my favorite food, people, and booze combined to make it an absolute blast!

In my search for a theme, I ran across "Forty is the New F-Word," and it was over. I LOVE a good F-word. It perfectly punctuates my point on certain occasions, and I am not ashamed to use it (sorry, not sorry). If you know, you know. I am solidly in my 40s now (45, to be exact), and while brainstorming F-words that I associated with this decade, I could not ignore fear. I admit that I was afraid of what might come.

There were many things that contributed to my fear. I was very active in my 30s and blessed with good health. I worried that would end. I mean, haven't you heard about joint pain, fatigue, swelling, and all those other things that happen as you age? Let's not forget wrinkles, age spots, and sagging skin (vain, I know, but it's my truth). By the end of the decade, Hubby and I would have adult children. What is not terrifying about having two teenage daughters and preparing them to leave the nest? My parents were getting older, and my precious grandmother had dementia and was getting more fragile every year. This is not the end of my list, but I am sure that some of this resonates with you. You can probably add to the list (feel free to speak your fears out loud; they are less scary that way)!

Fear can be debilitating. If you have anxiety, you know exactly what I mean. If not, I'm jealous. In case you are one of the lucky ones, let me put it simply. Fear is a giant pain in the ass. It can consume your thoughts and affect every aspect of your life, even your physical health. Overcoming it is hard work. It takes intentional thought and action. It takes dogged determination, and sometimes, you must fake it until you make it. I have done this, and although not the best plan, it worked. Here are some other things that worked for me:

1. **Reminders**: I placed sticky notes in places where I would see them daily.
   In the same essence, I set daily reminders on my phone. The notes were sometimes cheesy ("You can do it!"), sometimes scripture (Philippians 4:6-7, 2 Timothy 1:7, and Joshua 1:9), and sometimes badass ("You are never too old to set another goal or dream a new dream" – CS Lewis).

2. **Determination**: My girls were watching me. I had an example to set, and I was determined that fear would not be a word they associated with me.

3. **Encouragement**: I surrounded myself with family and friends who were supportive, but honest. I never want advice from someone who is likely to blow smoke up the proverbial hole. Instead, I need people I trust to be real all the time.

4. **Therapy**: I eventually found my way to therapy. It was several years after I turned 40, and after the tragic loss of my dad. I wish I had gone sooner. Ladies, if you don't have a therapist, you need one. More on that later...

Turning 40 felt scary, and I spent the last few years of my 30s dreading it. I made up all kinds of worries to support my fear. The thing I want to leave you with is this: Don't torture yourself! It's not that bad.

Truth time – so far, I love the person I've become in my 40s, and I'm excited about who I will be by the end of this decade.

CHAPTER 2

Family

A group of individuals living under one roof and usually under one head; a group of persons of common ancestry[2]

I DON'T KNOW ABOUT YOU, BUT I AM A FAMILY-ORIented girl. I was raised in a small town in the foothills of North Carolina, and I think I was related to most of the town. Before I can speak about family in my 40s, I must give you some background to describe how and why my roots grow deep. My parents divorced when I was four. I have a few memories from when they were still together, but not many. My parents remained friends and never spoke harshly about each other – at least not where I could hear. It was normal for both of my parents to attend birthdays, sporting events, award ceremonies, and dance recitals. I did not understand how rare this was until I was in high school.

    Both sides of my family are large, and we love each other. Both parents remarried, and I have amazing bonus families. When I was growing up, if there was a reason to gather, we did (especially if food was involved). Sunday lunches, holiday parties, birthdays, weddings, funerals, the list could go on and on. Everyone knew everyone else's business, and there were no secrets. If your cousins aren't like your siblings, I'm sorry. As I aged and great-grandparents passed away, the

---

2 Merriam-Webster. (n.d.). Family. In *Merriam-Webster.com dictionary*. Retrieved August 23, 2024, from https://www.merriam-webster.com/dictionary/family

frequency of extended family gatherings lessened, but let there be an emergency and see how quickly everyone shows up.

    I grew up living across the street from my grandparents and I spent as much time in their home as I did my own. My grandmother was a teacher's assistant and worked at the local elementary school. I rode to and from school with her daily and ate supper with them most nights. If they went on vacation, I packed my bags and went too. If they didn't want me to go, they had to sneak away, but they didn't do that often. My grandad died when I was 14, and it was the first major loss that I can remember. After that, I stayed with my grandmother for a while to make sure she was okay; though, I'm not sure who needed the other more. She and I were thick as thieves.

    Hubby and I met in high school but did not start dating until after. He was in the Marines, and I was in nursing school. It was a match made in heaven. We lived about 45 minutes away from my dad and bonus mom, but when we got married, they gave us land and we moved home. We built a home in a pasture behind them, and two daughters, four dogs, five cats, two goats, and one chameleon later (not all at the same time!), we are still going strong. This man is my rock, and he still makes my world go round. Our girls are amazing, and being their mom has been the best thing that has ever happened to me.

    Even though my overall family dynamic is wonderful, and the dynamic in my home is idyllic, we have our fair share of dysfunction. I feel sure most of you can relate. Toxic relationships exist within every family. If you fit into this category, rest assured that you are not alone. We all experience conflict within the familial unit at some point. In my immediate family alone, we had divorce, addiction, codependency, and financial distress, just to name a few. These types of stressors affect each of us in different ways, often depending on when we experience them. If you were the child of a narcissistic parent, you may have trouble maintaining your emotions or difficulty maintaining a healthy relationship as an adult. If you are an adult sibling of someone living with addiction, you may struggle with setting healthy boundaries, or you may grieve the relationship you have lost with that sibling. This topic is too big for the context of this book, but it cannot be ignored. How your family functions can affect you in every aspect of your life. Identifying the toxic relationships in your family and managing them appropriately is key to finding freedom in your life.

Although many things remain the same, big things have changed and that's what I'm here to talk about. If the 40s have a prevailing theme for me, it is change. At 41, I lost my dad and, a little over one year later, my grandmother. At 43, our then 18-year-old daughter spread her wings and landed 10 hours away at culinary school in New York. Sometimes change comes in the form of loss and loss is *hard*. Losing my dad was the hardest thing I've ever been through. Grieving is hard work, and it takes time and effort to move through the process. You may be going through a time of transition in your life, too. Divorce, empty nest, a career change, or a new baby may have your life feeling like total chaos. I am a different person than I was when I entered this decade. I've learned some difficult lessons, and I'd like to think I've grown from and through them.

The take-home point (for me, at least) is this – everyone is busy. We all have a lot on our plates. We have children who need us, spouses who need us, parents who need us, work, home, responsibilities, yada, yada, yada. Let me just get this over with. This might be hard to hear, but you need to hear it. Life is short. *We make time for the people that we love*. Date your spouse, plan a day (or weekend) with your favorite cousins, have dinner with your sibling, or do something fun with your kids. Family is forever, but you do not have endless time on this earth with them. Do your best to make the best of it. You are in your 40s, ladies. Now is the time to decide what (and who) is important to you and spend as much time making memories with them as possible.

CHAPTER 3

Friendship

The state of being friends (one attached to another by affection or esteem; one that is not hostile; a favored companion)[34]

I AM LUCKY ENOUGH TO HAVE FRIENDS THAT ARE FAMily and family that are friends. Some have moved away and some live close. Some I see twice a year and others I see every week. They've been with me through thick and thin. These types of friends know things about us that no one else knows, and they still come around. A good friend is worth their weight in gold, and I've never appreciated them more than I do now.

Friendships change as we travel through life. *It can be difficult to maintain friendships through the different stages of life.* If you are a mom or are friends with a mom, you understand what I'm saying. No one is busier than a parent. Attending ball games, planning birthday parties, scheduling medical appointments, working (in the home or in the office), cleaning the house, cooking dinner, homework, volunteering at school, and keeping everyone sane takes a lot of time. Frankly, years can pass where it feels like that is all you do. Friends that stick around when you don't have time for them are

---

3 Merriam-Webster. (n.d.). Friendship. In *Merriam-Webster.com dictionary*. Retrieved August 23, 2024, from https://www.merriam-webster.com/dictionary/friendship

4 Merriam-Webster. (n.d.). Friend. In *Merriam-Webster.com dictionary*. Retrieved August 23, 2024, from https://www.merriam-webster.com/dictionary/friend

friends that will stick around for life. Appreciate them; keep them; make time for them. You will need them.

I cannot continue this chapter without saying that Hubby is my absolute best friend. He knows everything about me and is the first person I call when I have something to share. We were friends in high school for several years before we dated. Our relationship is grounded in the fact that we actually like each other, but it has not always been easy. Our friendship is a result of intention. We have worked to carve out time to be alone together over the years. Many of us are near the stage in our lives where our children are leaving the nest. It's important for you and your partner to still know and like each other when this happens. Plan date nights and entire weekends whenever possible. If the kids are still young, pay a sitter or call the grandparents and spend some one-on-one time with your partner. If you are like me and your kids are older, there's no better time than right now to befriend your partner. Keeping that friendship alive is what will carry your relationship when times are hard.

My two best friends have been lifelong friends. One was my first friend in kindergarten, and the other was my first new friend in high school. It doesn't matter how much time passes between seeing (or even talking to) each other, we pick up right where we left off every single time. They feel like home to me. These two women know about all the things that made me who I am. They have been there with me through thick and thin and they understand me. If you have friends like this, you understand. If they need me, I am there. No questions asked.

Just as I have friends that are family, I have family that are my friends. One of my closest adult friends is my first cousin. She also feels like home to me. No one else knows you like the people that you had sleepovers with at your grandparents' house. When my dad was sick, she was the person that brought me the most comfort. She is one of the first people I call when I need to be talked off a ledge or when I have exciting news. I trust her to tell me like it is and to lift me up when I am down.

Some of our friends are only meant to be with us for a certain period of time. If you are a parent, it is likely that some of your friends are connected to your children. You became friends because your kids were in the same class or on the same team. Maybe you bonded over club sports travel or science fair assignments. These friends are no less special because their time was limited in your life. You filled a void in each other that you never knew was empty, and these friendships often fade away the same way they entered your life, slowly and gently.

Many of us also have work friends. These are your people at work. The ones you share a knowing side-eye with during that meeting that goes on forever, and the ones who appreciate a well-placed disgruntled employee reel. Often, they aren't the people you hang out with on the weekend, but your friendship is no less important. When they aren't at work, the day and/or the workload seems never-ending. In today's work culture, they may only be in your life for a short period of time, but they often leave you better than they found you. Some of my most appreciated friendships were originally work colleagues.

If I leave you with nothing else in this chapter, I want you to know that it's important for you to have friends, and it will take work to maintain some of those friendships. You might not always be able to dedicate time to a girls' day, but you can spend a few minutes checking in with them. Send a text to see if they are okay. Let them know if you thought about them today. We all need a reminder that we are important to someone else. Any time you can, plan a day (or evening) to get together, even if you have to put it on the calendar a month or two in advance. Investing time in your friendships will be good for you. When life is hard, they will lift you up, and trust me, sometimes life is going to be hard.

CHAPTER 4

Forgiveness

The act of forgiving[5]; an intentional decision to let go of negative emotions

THIS ONE MIGHT BE TOUGH. WHICH ONE OF Y'ALL ARE holding a grudge? Don't bother lying because you're only lying to yourself. I'm not going to sugarcoat it; forgiveness is hard. I should know I'm from the South, and our grudges last for generations. The truth of the matter is that holding on to anger, hurt, or resentment only serves to hurt you. It doesn't have any effect on the person it's directed toward. It is time to start letting stuff go.

When I first started seeing a counselor a few years ago, I remember boasting about how I was exceptional at avoiding things that made me feel uncomfortable. I thought this was a strength of mine. Hahaha. I was *wrong*. I prefer to live in harmony. I don't like to be angry or carry things around that feel burdensome. Some would call me conflict-avoidant, but I don't like labels. If we all lived in Wendy's World, life would be much better and happier. At least, that's what I thought.

This might make you think that forgiveness is easy for me; however, that is so far from the truth that it's laughable. Because of this preference for avoidance, I used to box unpleasant things up

---

5 Merriam-Webster. (n.d.). Forgiveness. In *Merriam-Webster.com dictionary*. Retrieved August 23, 2024, from https://www.merriam-webster.com/dictionary/forgiveness

neatly, tie it with a pretty bow, and store it under lock and key deep in the recesses of my brain. I was an expert avoider. (Again…this is not a good thing.) Avoidance is **NOT** forgiveness. In fact, I would theorize that avoidance leads to resentment, which is the opposite of forgiveness. Is anyone else reading this an expert avoider? Good. I knew I wasn't alone, but I am proof that you can change, and that it's good for you!

All the peace that I thought I was cultivating for myself was really only peaceful for others. Instead of peace, avoidance brought me stress, anger, resentment, fear, and shame, all of the negative emotions. I never forgave anyone because I never openly held anyone accountable (including myself). Counseling helped me to realize that this is toxic. In fact, my counselor compared my brain to an episode of *Hoarders* and told me I was holding onto all the negative interactions that I didn't want to address. She also told me that if I didn't stop, one day, I would no longer be able to store any emotions, including the good ones. In case you didn't know, holding on to anger is dangerous to your mental and physical health.

I had a lot of unboxing to do before I could get back to a healthy way of managing difficult emotions. The hardest part for me was deciding where to start. I was holding on to a lot of things, y'all. I had a lot of forgiving to do – starting with myself. Here are a few of the things that helped me get started:

1. Stop boxing up anything new. This means less to unpack later. I had to remind myself of the following daily (you can call it my mantra if you will):
    a. You are a grown-ass woman. You can handle anything that is thrown your way today.
    b. The best way to address something is with honesty.
    c. Finally, to quote the great Dr. Seuss, "Be who you are and say what you feel because those who mind don't matter and those who matter don't mind."

2. Figure out if any of those unpleasant things are attached to people whom you love and who love you. If so, unbox and deal with those first. These are people who should be important to you, and they should get the *real* you, not a watered-down version. If they are worthy of your love, then they are also worthy of your real feelings.

3. If any of those unpleasant things are attached to people or things that do not matter, let them go. They are cluttering up your emotions and making you more unavailable for the ones that do matter. Why are you holding on to them in the first place?

Real talk: most of us need to start by forgiving ourselves, but this can be the most difficult of all. Why is it that we are harder on ourselves than we are on anyone else? How can we expect to love others if we cannot love ourselves? I've said it a few times already, but I will say it again. We are in our 40s, y'all. It's way past time for us to start loving ourselves. We owe it to our partners, children, parents, and friends, but mostly, we owe it to us. We need to become the best version of ourselves, and that can only begin to happen when we find a way to forgive ourselves and others.

CHAPTER 5

Function

The action for which a person or thing is specially fitted or used or for which a thing exists (PURPOSE)
To be in action (operate)[6]

THE ABOVE DEFINITION LIKENS "FUNCTION" TO PURpose, and isn't that what we would all like to figure out? What is our purpose in this life? What were we born to do? I mean, maybe I am the only one in my 40s that really isn't sure, but I believe this is not the case. I also think it's worthy to consider the second definition (the verb). How do we function on the daily? Are we getting up, going through the motions, going to bed, and repeating, or do we function with purpose? Ooooo…I hit my own nerve with that one.

How many of you can honestly raise your hand and say that you are doing exactly what you are supposed to be doing in this life, and you know this without a doubt? Kudos to you ladies! (Will you message me and let me in on the secret?) I am not this person. I used to tell people that I had no idea what I wanted to be when I grew up. I mean, I think I want to be someone who sits on the beach with a margarita anytime she wants, but that's not in the cards for me just yet. All jokes aside, I think that I am starting to find my next purpose and I hope this chapter helps you to seek or find yours.

---

[6] Merriam-Webster. (n.d.). Function. In *Merriam-Webster.com dictionary*. Retrieved August 23, 2024, from https://www.merriam-webster.com/dictionary/function

For the past 20 years, my primary function was raising children and being a good partner to my husband. In fact, I often told my daughters that my most important job as a parent was to help shape them into adults that other people wanted to be around and who make positive contributions to society. It felt like my highest calling, but they are now grown (or nearly so), so what now? Many of you are in the same boat, almost/already empty nesters and now what? Honestly, I am unsure what comes next for me, but I'm working on it. It's a slow and often grueling process, but I'm not getting any younger, so I'm putting my back into it and forging a new path.

Another of my functions for my entire adult life was being a nurse. Through nursing, I found my way to women's health, and this is where I found my second purpose. My youngest was so offended when she first realized that I did pelvic exams and pap smears every day. In fact, she asked me, "Why in the world do you want to do that?" My answer then, and my answer now, is that women should not be afraid to take care of their bodies. If I can provide care in a way that makes someone feel comfortable in an impossible situation, then maybe that person will seek care again when she needs it. Let's be honest: who wants to throw their legs in stirrups and have someone swabbing around down there? Nobody, that's who, but it's important for us to take preventive measures to ensure our health. I digress here, but this is important, so I'm going to go ahead and do it. Ladies, we must be as healthy as possible to fulfill our purpose in this world. If you can't remember the last time you had a pap smear, breast exam, or mammogram (you are 40 and it's time), then you probably need to schedule an appointment. Here are some numbers you should remember:

> **FIVE**: You should get a Pap smear every 5 years (if your last one was normal and you tested negative for the human papillomavirus).
>
> **THREE**: You should have a breast exam *at least* every three years.

ONE: You need a mammogram every 1-2 years, depending on your personal risk factors. Okay…I'm jumping off that soap box before I start preaching at you.

I almost skipped this next part because it steps on my own toes a bit. We're going to talk about the other definition of function for a minute. If I'm being honest (and we already know total transparency is the theme of this book), I do not function with purpose every day. Some days, I sit down at the end of the day and feel accomplished with the things I checked off the to-do list that day. Some days, I coast through the day, accomplishing a few things but not really interested in being productive or purposeful. I am also guilty of occasionally lying around like a lump of coal all day. For me, it's about balance. Actually, the days I rest are usually designed that way. They come after I have functioned at full capacity for several days or weeks in a row, and I need a day of rest more than I need a Diet Pepsi, and y'all, I LOVE some Diet Pepsi. We do not have to function with purpose every day. It's okay to rest. It's okay to be on autopilot some days. What's important is that you remember to give yourself grace on the days you aren't at 100% and pat yourself on the back on the days that you are.

Do you wonder about your purpose? Have you ever sat down and really thought about it? Do you think you know what it is? Are you already living/doing it, or do you need to start working toward that purpose? Either way, we should look at this like it's now or never. We owe it to ourselves and our loved ones to function at our highest capacity, and there's no better day than today to get started. This is not intended to stress you out. Instead, it's a reminder that you are amazing and you have more to offer now than you did a decade ago. Go out and offer that shit up on a platter, my friends.

CHAPTER 6

Fatigue

Weariness or exhaustion from labor, exertion, or stress[7]

WHEW, FRIENDS. I DON'T KNOW ABOUT YOU, BUT I DID not need the definition for this chapter. I know about fatigue; I have felt it deep in my bones. Some days, it seems like I am barely able to get through the day. *If I can just make it until bedtime, it will be okay.* Does this sound familiar? We have all been there and for many different reasons. We are going to spend some time discussing a few common reasons for fatigue in our 40s and what we can do to make it better.

Hello, menopause. I'd say it's nice to meet you, but it would be a lie. Menopause occurs after women go for one entire year without having a period and happens at an average age of 51 years. This means that some women will experience it at an earlier age, and some may not experience it until much later. Perimenopause is the period of time leading up to menopause. It often begins in the 40s and may last for as long as ten years before completely transitioning to menopause. Did you know that fatigue is generally more common in women than in men (insert eye roll here)? As if we have time for that…right? Add in the frequently shifting hormones associated with perimenopause and the common symptoms of hot flashes, night

---

[7] Merriam-Webster. (n.d.). Fatigue. In *Merriam-Webster.com dictionary*. Retrieved August 23, 2024, from https://www.merriam-webster.com/dictionary/fatigue

sweats, and insomnia, and you have the perfect recipe for fatigue. If this sounds familiar, there are some things you can do to help.

1. Talk to your healthcare provider. You might have to start the conversation and be persistent. Many of the symptoms of perimenopause can also be symptoms of other common illnesses. There is also no blood test or widely used tool to help diagnose perimenopause. Your provider needs to hear about all of your symptoms, ALL of them, to fit the pieces together and make this diagnosis.

2. If they tell you it's just a normal part of aging and you are going to have to adjust, just leave. It's time to find someone else to take care of you. There are plenty of things you can do to help with your symptoms, decrease your fatigue, and greatly improve your quality of life. If you need to find a new provider, you can find a list of certified menopause providers on the North American Menopause Society's website[8].

3. Consider revamping your diet and exercise routine. As our hormones shift, we often need something different than what worked for us in our 30s. There's tons of information out there about this; just make sure you are using trusted sources.

Illness is another common reason for fatigue. Living with any long-term illness, whether it is mental or physical, can cause fatigue. Stress, anxiety, and depression often lead to fatigue, which is worsened by the poor sleep that many experience when struggling with these conditions. Fatigue can be a symptom of a number of underlying health conditions, such as diabetes, heart disease, or a thyroid disorder, just to name a few. It can also be a product of the effort it takes to care for yourself in the presence of that health condition. Regardless of the reason, if you have a health condition and are

---

8 https://www.menopause.org/

experiencing increased or persistent fatigue, you need to discuss this with your healthcare provider.

Many of us are caregivers. We are raising children, caring for aging family members, and often burning the candle at both ends to do both. Add the responsibilities of work, home, and social commitments, and OF COURSE you are tired. Girl. Some days you are stretched so thin, we could see right through you. Imagine this (I'm betting you won't have to): you waited up for your teenager to get home from a date, so you went to bed late. Then, your third grader wakes you up at 2:00 am with a sore throat and a fever. Finally, you have an 8:00 am meeting that you cannot miss, and you spent the rest of the night trying to figure out who was going to stay home with the sick kiddo so you could just get through that meeting. You need a nap, but when in the world are you going to take one? It's another full day of responsibilities, with the addition of a trip to the doctor's office and some extra snuggles with your sick little love. If you don't have children, insert the dog heaving on the bed at 2:00 am instead. I know you get the point. Sometimes it feels like we go through days upon days of this, never catching a break. Do yourself and all your loved ones a favor and schedule some time for self-care. If you are exhausted, your immune system cannot work as well as it should, and you might just find *yourself* with a sore throat and fever, and you certainly don't have time for that.

There are many other reasons you may experience fatigue, but in the interest of keeping your attention I'm going to skip ahead to what you can do about it. The first step is to talk to your healthcare provider. Some amount of fatigue is normal (especially if you recently experienced the situation in the previous paragraph) and doesn't necessitate a visit to the clinic, but if you have been utterly exhausted day after day, it is worth the trip.

If you haven't had any blood work recently, that would be a good place to start. We can check for many of the common causes of fatigue with some simple labs. Unfortunately, perimenopause isn't one of them. There aren't any great tests that confirm this diagnosis.

For this reason, it's important for you to be open and honest with your healthcare provider. You have to be willing to start the conversation about it. Even the best healthcare provider cannot read your mind.

Becoming the healthiest version of yourself goes a long way to improve fatigue. This means taking your medications when you are supposed to (not when you want to), going to bed when you need to (sleep is *IMPORTANT* and deserves an entire book), and taking care of your physical and mental fitness. Just because we are 40-something does not mean we have to be tired, but this is where you must take control. Whether you want to hear it or not, a healthy diet and an appropriate amount of exercise have many more benefits than changing your clothing size. Keep reading to hear more!

CHAPTER 7

Fitness

The quality or state of being fit (sound mentally and physically)[9]

IF YOU WERE TEMPTED TO SKIP THIS CHAPTER, YOU are not alone. Many of us prefer to be like an ostrich and stick our heads in the sand when we feel threatened, and the word fitness carries a whole basketful of trauma. In this chapter, we are not only going to dive into physical fitness, but we are also going to spend some time discussing mental fitness. Both are imperative to being your best self, especially in your 40s.

Let's jump right into physical fitness. I've been a nurse since 2001 and a nurse practitioner since 2009, but I've been into fitness for as long as I can remember. You do not have to look like a bodybuilder to be fit. You also don't have to be thin. Let me say that again. You DO NOT have to be thin to be fit. I will go ahead and put this out there, and I am prepared to get blasted for it by some health and fitness professionals. I don't care about your body mass index (BMI). The powers that be decided that a normal BMI is between 18-25. Body mass index is determined by your height and your weight. Only those two factors go into it. You might have 12% body fat, but your BMI may be 29. In fact, bodybuilders often have incredibly low body fat, yet they have a high BMI because of their muscle mass. The

---

9 Merriam-Webster. (n.d.). Fitness. In *Merriam-Webster.com dictionary*. Retrieved August 23, 2024, from https://www.merriam-webster.com/dictionary/fitness

number on the scale *does not* determine your fitness level or your risk of developing heart disease. I care more about what your diet looks like and whether or not you exercise.

Nutrition is important because food is fuel. We must fuel our minds and our bodies, and this becomes even more important as we age. I will never ever encourage cutting out any food group completely. I believe in and personally practice "all things in moderation". All food groups have their purpose. We need carbs, and fat, and protein to function at our highest level mentally and physically. How much of those we need depends on several individual factors and may change from day to day and will certainly change as we near menopause. I personally, also need something sweet every day. Nutritional experts may argue that I do not, in fact, need something sweet every day. They would be correct; however, I am not diabetic, I exercise consistently, and chocolate is life.

Exercise is not a dirty word. The key is to stop thinking about it like it's another chore or something else that you must do. Exercise does not have to be miserable. For example, I love to dance. I was a dancer growing up and then later taught dance for nearly 20 years. Dance is an excellent aerobic activity, but it does not feel like exercise to me. It is a great way for me to release stress and get moving, and if I really get into a groove, I can burn a lot of calories in a short amount of time. Conversely, I HATE to run. If running were the only way to exercise, I would never exercise again. The entire time I'm running, I'm miserable. I don't know about you, but I'm not going to keep doing something that makes me miserable. Find the type of activity doesn't feel like work to you and it will be easier to add it into your daily life. It may even become a priority.

You should aim for 150 minutes of exercise each week[10]. KEEP READING! I know that sounds like a lot, but that is a total of 150

---

10 American Heart Association (2024). *American Heart Association recommendations for physical activity in adults and kids.* https://www.heart.org/en/healthy-living/fitness/fitness-basics/aha-recs-for-physical-activity-in-adults#:~:text=Recommendations%20for%20Adults,Recommendations%20for%20Kids

minutes in 7 days. If you do the math, that is only a little more than 21 minutes each day. You can divide that up any way you want. If you have time to do 45 minutes today and only 15 tomorrow, that is still 60 minutes in 2 days. Get outside and take a walk on your lunch break (sunshine and fresh air are good for the soul). Practice yoga when you wake up. Weight-bearing exercise is important for our bones as we get older and can help prevent osteoporosis. This includes any type of exercise that requires being on your feet; even better if you can add some free weights a few times a week. Our bodies are getting older, and it is more important than ever to protect their function. If we don't use it, we will certainly lose it, and no one else can do this for us. Get up and get moving, friends!

Now, let's discuss mental fitness. This is a loaded topic and, like many others in this book, one that deserves an entire book of its own. Fortunately, there are several great ones already written so I'm just going to speak to a few things. *You cannot be well if you are not mentally well.* There are so many factors that go into one's mental wellness: past trauma, current trauma, body image, chemicals (both internal and external), brain function, stress, and fatigue, just to name a few. There's a good chance that many of you could put a checkmark next to all of those things mentioned in the previous sentence and add several more. My question is, what are you doing about it? If your answer is nothing, I'm here to give you permission to change that.

Story time. I have anxiety, and I've had it my entire life. I'm pretty sure that I was an anxiety-ridden toddler, but I know for a fact that worry was a primary feeling for me as early as kindergarten. I worried about everything, but way back then, we weren't as in touch with mental health as we are now, so it wasn't something one talked about. I had no idea this wasn't something that everyone else experienced until I got much older. Even though I had vast personal experience with anxiety, I had never been depressed until after my dad passed away. Y'all, I am a healthcare professional and did not recognize that I was depressed. One year after he died, I finally went to counseling because a great friend lovingly bullied me into scheduling an appointment. It was another year after that when my counselor said to me one day, "I've seen you depressed, and you are not there now." Talk about an aha moment. I never gave myself permission to feel my feelings until that day.

Before my personal experience, I believed that everyone probably needed a counselor, but I never got around to seeing one myself. Now, I am an avid advocate for therapy, have encouraged many of my family members to go and recommend it to all my friends and patients. Ladies, it's an hour (or two) of your time when you get to talk about you. You (or your insurance) are paying for it, so you might as well make the best of it. It may take several attempts to find someone you feel comfortable with. Keep trying! I got lucky and hit the jackpot right away; maybe the universe was rewarding me for *finally* making an appointment.

Many of us struggle with feeling selfish when we take time to care for ourselves. One thing I have learned from my counselor is that you cannot pour from an empty cup. If you always give of yourself and never take time for self-care (or to refill your love tank, as she says), you will eventually flame out. You can only run on fumes for so long. By the time I finally went to counseling, my tank was far past empty. I had a lot of baggage to unpack and I'm betting that you probably do too. Self-care is not just important; it's imperative to your physical and mental health. What are you doing to take care of yourself today?

Finally, let's talk about drugs. I don't mean the kind that could get you locked up for the next decade. I'm talking about the kind that you may need to address your mental health. Are you struggling with anxiety or depression? If so, you are not alone. More than one-third of the adult population is suffering from some type of anxiety or depression[11]. If you didn't have it before the pandemic, odds are you might have it now. Please don't continue to suffer, and don't suffer alone! Therapy is effective but may not be enough by itself. There are many medications (both prescription and supplements) out there that can help balance out your imbalances and help you be the best version of yourself. Pro tip: please do not try your partner's medication. Just because it works for them, does not mean it's what *you* need. Schedule an appointment with your healthcare provider or ask your counselor for a recommendation (if they are not a psychiatrist, they cannot prescribe medication). Be open and honest at your appointment. There's a good chance you will be asked to complete a questionnaire that helps determine how much you are struggling. That questionnaire helps your provider know what type of treatment to recommend, so fill it out honestly. They cannot treat you appropriately if you aren't real about your struggles.

Ladies, we must take care of ourselves. We belong to a generation that may find it hard to do, but it is vital to living our best lives. My body hurts sometimes when I wake up (and not in the good, sore from a great workout kind of way), and my brain gets tired and foggy easier than it used to. We are NOT old, but there's a good chance most of us are beginning to experience some physical and mental signs of aging. We have to do all that we can now to ensure that we can actually live and not only age. Now…put this book down for a bit, schedule your therapy appointment, and go outside for a walk!

---

11 KFF (2023, Mar 10). Latest federal data show that young people are more likely than older adults to be experiencing symptoms of anxiety or depression. Retrieved August 25, 2024 from https://www.kff.org/mental-health/press-release/latest-federal-data-show-that-young-people-are-more-likely-than-older-adults-to-be-experiencing-symptoms-of-anxiety-or-depression/ - :~:text=The mental health and substance,to 32.3 percent in 2023

CHAPTER 8

Failure

A state of inability to perform a normal function
A lack of success; a failing in business
A falling short[12]

THERE ARE MANY WAYS IN WHICH FAILURE CAN BE defined. I'm going to go out on a limb and say that what I consider failure in my life may not be failure in yours, or vice versa. How we personally define failure can be determined by how we were raised, how we define success, or even how we perceive others' definitions of success. I'm betting that none of you have reached this point in your life without experiencing failure. In fact, I dreaded writing this chapter because I have experienced my fair share of it, and it's not always fun to think about.

Many times, we fail by not even trying. I was terrified to write this book. "What if no one likes it? What if people think I'm a fraud? What if it's terrible?" This is way out of my comfort zone. If you want me to give a presentation to a room full of people about something in the nursing profession, I'm your girl. Of course, I was afraid to bomb the first time I presented, but I was blessed with the gift of gab. I can talk to anyone and everyone… and I do! (Just ask my kids.) I grew up dancing on a stage in front of hundreds of people. Being

---

12 Merriam-Webster. (n.d.). Failure. In *Merriam-Webster.com dictionary*. Retrieved August 23, 2024, from https://www.merriam-webster.com/dictionary/failure

in front of a lot of people is invigorating to me. This book, though, is *scary*. What made me finally start writing it is letting go of what anyone else might think of it. Even if it doesn't sell one copy, it is still a personal success because I finished it.

Without asking, I know that you have experienced failure. In fact, I believe there is no way you have reached your 40s without failing on some level. You may have experienced failure at work (didn't get that promotion that you wanted), failure in a relationship (divorce), or failure at meeting a personal goal (hello, New Year's resolutions). Before we can keep going in this chapter, I need you to do something that might be difficult. Spend a few minutes thinking back over some of the things you consider to be your biggest failures in life, then think about where you are now. Did those failures help you to get to where you are? What did you learn from them? How can you share what you learned with others who may be going through something similar?

While writing this, I spent some time reflecting on the different types of failure I've experienced throughout my life. I am nothing if not honest, so in all transparency, I'm going to share a few of what I consider my biggest failures with you.

1. **Parenting**. If you are a parent reading this book, I feel positive that I could leave it at that one word, and you would understand. I've lost count of how many times I failed as a parent. I could fill this book with all of the things that I did wrong and all of the regrets I have. Somehow, amidst the many failures, we still managed to raise two strong-willed, independent-thinking, kind young women. Often, we forget that kids are resilient, and if we love them unconditionally and do our best for them, the failures aren't as dramatic as we may feel they are.

2. **Settling.** Another of what I consider to be one of my biggest failures is settling for what is comfortable instead of chasing a dream or going after something that felt scary or intimidating. Many of us do this because change is hard. It is difficult for me to let go of things, and I never want to burn a bridge, even if it should have been set ablaze years ago. I am working to move past these issues and to grow through them. If I've learned anything in the first five years of my 40s, it's that it's never too late to try again or even try for the first time.

If you've reflected on things you consider to be failures in your life, now's the time to decide how you are going to learn from them, change your approach, and try again. There's no time like the present. You cannot fail without trying, but you also cannot succeed. Being afraid to go after something you want because you are afraid to fail will never lead you to where you want to be. What does it mean to *you* to have success? Are you trying to measure up to someone else's definition? If so, you should really stop that…like right now. Say this out loud: *it does not matter what anyone else thinks.* Go ahead and say it again, several times, if you need to. Make yourself a sticky note and put it on your bathroom mirror. It does not matter what anyone else thinks. If we spend our lives trying to measure up to someone else, we will fail time and again. It is time for us to reframe failure in our minds. Let's work to redefine it into something positive. Without failure, we cannot have growth!

CHAPTER 9

Fierce

Marked by unrestrained zeal or vehemence
Furiously active or determined
Wild or menacing in appearance
Having or expressing bold confidence or style[13]

I'M NOT SURE ABOUT YOU, BUT I HAVE ALWAYS FELT fierce on the inside. I *felt* that way but did not always have the courage to act on it. This is yet another reason I love the me that I have become in my 40s. Every one of these definitions apply to me on any given day, and sometimes, all at the same time. I feel sure many of you can relate. What does it mean to be fierce? To me, it's definitely a compliment, and it's something I strive to be daily.

I'm not sure anyone would have labeled me as fierce when I was younger. I was a compliant, peaceful rule-follower for most of my life. I avoided trouble like the plague. When I think back, I can remember times when I wanted to break that mold, but I had been raised not to rock the boat. "What would they think?" was one of my grandmother's favorite ways to reign me back in when I got a little wild. Despite her best efforts, or maybe even because of them, I have become a fierce adult, but it has taken years, actually most of my adult life, to allow myself to be bold.

---

[13] Merriam-Webster. (n.d.). Fierce. In *Merriam-Webster.com dictionary*. Retrieved August 23, 2024, from https://www.merriam-webster.com/dictionary/fierce

Why do we let others tame our spirit? As young girls, we are often expected to be meek. Many of us were taught from a young age to be quiet, to be seen and not heard, or to give in to keep the peace. Sometimes, we were taught by example; it's how we saw the women in our lives behave. Sometimes, it was a survival technique, and I'm not here to make you feel bad about that. I am here; however, to tell you that you don't have to finish your life that way. I am also here to remind you that young women often learn from us. I want my daughters (and my patients) to see me as a strong, capable woman. The thing is, I don't just want them to see me that way. I want to *be* that way. I want to be the lamppost to guide their way. Ladies, I believe we are the generation that will change this for our daughters. We can show them how to be kind and considerate while still being bold and kick-ass. Those traits can *and should* coexist.

The second and third definitions above were "marked by unrestrained zeal or vehemence" and "furiously active and determined". I like to think that by this decade of our lives, we have learned some things. We should know better, and we must DO and BE better. My lifelong best friend is setting the standard for this. She is one of the most compassionate people I know. She's also one of the most relentless advocates I've ever met, even if it brings her suffering. She *defines* fierce at 40. She has taken the time to educate herself about social injustice and has become a voice for equity. Although this has taken a toll on her mentally and physically, she has been steadfast in her quest to bring awareness. We could all learn from her. If we sit and remain quiet when we see wrong in this world, how will things ever change? We must start rocking the boat.

Let's all take a minute to think about the third definition listed above: "Wild or menacing in appearance". I want to be wild in appearance sometimes (maybe even most of the time). It's obviously in my nature, my natural hair tells that story all by itself. I spent years trying to tame it, but once I finally gave in to the curls and waves, I found out that I actually liked my hair a little wild and crazy. My stylist calls it "Wendy's hair." Fierce is a state of mind and I want to live there all the time. When others look at me, I want them to see that I am strong and that I DO NOT desire to fit into any mold. We are women; hear us roar!

We should refuse to let anyone else define who we are or decide what our future will entail. We should have primary input in what our lives look like. Majority rules, and in this case, the majority is one. It's time to open the door and usher out anything that is holding you back. It's time to be fierce!

CHAPTER 10

Fashion

The prevailing style (as in dress) during a particular time; a distinctive or peculiar and often habitual manner or way[14]

DO YOU HAVE YOUR OWN STYLE? DO YOU KNOW WHAT you like or what makes *you* feel good when you wear it? If not, it's time to figure it out. You're not getting any younger, and, odds are, you have entered a time in your life when you really do not care what anyone else thinks. My style is heavily influenced by my state of mind when I get dressed, with a side helping of "Where am I going and what will I be doing?".

We are lucky, ladies. We are living in an era where clothes are cut for every figure. Tall, curvy, straight, pear, apple, it doesn't matter. You can find something that works for you, and that makes you feel good. The trick is to know what you like and to fill your drawers and shelves with items that fit the bill. If you haven't cleaned out your closet in a decade, it's wayyyyy past time for that. Go ahead and stop reading. Use whatever free time you have today to go and get rid of anything that's too small, too large, or too uncomfortable. If you haven't worn it in a year, you likely will not wear it this year. Shoes, bras, and underwear too. I mean, use discretion. If you don't have the funds to replace all your underwear this week, only get rid

---

14 Merriam-Webster. (n.d.). Fashion. In *Merriam-Webster.com dictionary*. Retrieved August 23, 2024, from https://www.merriam-webster.com/dictionary/fashion

of the worst of the bunch. Those thongs that you haven't worn in a decade, trash. (Please don't take them to the local donation center.) Those shoes that pinch your toes or hurt your heels, out. That shirt that makes you feel frumpy, dunzo. You get the idea.

It is not easy for me to say these things. I am a hoarder of clothes, shoes, bags, and all the pretty things. My husband would concur, so don't get him started. Until recently, I was hanging on to jeans that I haven't been able to comfortably wear in 5 years because they were once my favorite pair, and what if I'm able to lose these 10 pounds? OUT ladies! They are taking up valuable space in your closet that would be better served by something that makes you feel good. Squeezing into those jeans and not being able to eat while wearing them is a sign that it's time to go shopping.

I believe in supporting local small businesses and I also believe in investing in signature pieces that will last. For that reason, you will find a lot of variety in my closet. It's not about price; it's about comfort, style, wearability, and longevity. I have an inordinate number of black leggings. It's ridiculous really; however, I wear them all, AND I don't have to spend as much free time doing laundry because I'm not likely to run out. Win! I love to look sexy when I'm going out with my hubby, and I love to look stylish when I'm going out with friends. Equally, I love to be comfortable when lounging at home or traveling. I appreciate looking professional when at work, and I adore shoes, but only if they don't hurt my feet. I'm too old for that mess. We do not have to suffer to look good!

Just because we are in our 40s doesn't mean that we must dress like our grandmothers. If you want to and you like that look, I'm not throwing shade. You do you! My oldest daughter went through a phase in high school where she bought most of her clothes at the local Goodwill and they were brands that I also found in my grandmother's closet. She looked cute, but I would not have been able to pull that off. Don't dress your age. What does that even mean? *Dress for you. Period.* If you like crop tops and leggings, flaunt it. If you're into blazers and jeans, I want to dress like you when I grow up.

If you rock pencil skirts and stilettos, kudos my friend. I have a tall, beautiful friend that wears the best heels and I'm always in awe of how she walks without breaking a heel (or her neck). She owns those heels, and that is what makes it work for her.

I will say it again for those in the back. Wear what makes you feel good; what makes you happy. Life is too short to worry about what anyone else thinks or to dress for anyone else.

CHAPTER 11

Feeling Good

*This needs no definition!
This is going to be fun, y'all. I've been waiting on this chapter,
and trust me, you have too.*

LET'S TALK ABOUT SEX. BACK IN AN EARLIER CHAPter, we learned that change is the mantra for our 40s. That applies here too, but I have exciting news for you. You may have heard that women reach their sexual peak in their 30s. While that is true, the good news is that we can continue to have a high level of sexual function until the mid-50's, and there is no reason to think it must stop then. You might be shaking your head or saying some things under your breath while you read this, but just be patient. We are going to work through this together.

First of all, let me raise your eyebrows. You don't need a partner to have an orgasm. I said what I said. Did that word make you cringe? If so, I'm going to need you to say it out loud. Go ahead and practice saying it (no need to whisper if you're reading this in a public place…*FIERCE,* remember?). If you are still cringing, be prepared for a permanent blush after reading the rest of this chapter. If you don't know how to pleasure yourself, how do you expect someone else to figure it out? Ladies, we are in our forties. We are mature and capable and strong and intelligent. We need to understand our bodies and know them better than anyone else.

If you've never looked at yourself with a mirror, go get one now, and I'll walk you through this. We all have similar parts, and all of us have three holes. Don't laugh...some women don't know that. This is why the mirror is important. The top hole is your urethra. Don't stick anything up there. It will hurt, and it will not bring pleasure. It may also cause a raging urinary tract infection, and none of us have time for that. The very back hole is the anus, it connects to the intestine, and it's where the poop comes out (sexy, right?). The middle hole is the vagina. It's important for a lot of reasons, most famously for being the baby tunnel. It's the home of the infamous G-spot, and it's the origin of some women's orgasms. Now, look above the urethra (top hole), and you will find the clitoris. It is a bundle of nerves and is typically very sensitive. It is the origin of most women's orgasms. Fun fact: the clitoris can be as long as 4.5 inches[15]. Yes, ladies, you read that right! You can only see the tip of it. The clitoris is actually very similar to the penis and has a shaft and a glans. The glans is the part you can see in the mirror.

Now that we have that out of the way, let's get to the nitty gritty. Do you know how *you* orgasm? What makes you get there? If not, figure it out. It's important. It might not be the same as it was 15 years ago. It might take longer, or more foreplay, or anal pressure (hey...this is a judgment-free zone!). I am a firm believer that everyone needs a B.O.T (battery-operated toy). They come in all shapes, sizes, colors, and abilities and you shouldn't knock them until you try them. There are some that are for the clitoris, some that are for the vagina or anus, and some that are for all three at the same time. Some pulsate, others rotate, others vibrate, and some don't have any superpowers, but they all serve a purpose. Invest in a good one and figure out what makes you shout. Then, share that important information with your partner if you have one.

I hear from women all the time who have noticed decreased sexual desire. There are many reasons this happens. One of the most

---

15 Pauls, R.N. (2015). Anatomy of the clitoris and the female sexual response. *Clinical Anatomy, 28*(3), 376-384. https://doi.org/10.1002/ca.22524

common is stress. If you have a long list of things that you need to do, sexy time is probably not at the top of your priority list. If you have young kids a busy job, or there are dishes in the sink, you might find it difficult to turn off your thoughts long enough to get turned on. If this is the case for you, it might help to put it on your calendar. Pick a day of the week and save some time to get it on. If you and your partner are always exhausted at the end of the day, don't pencil it in at bedtime. That's setting yourself up for failure. You know your schedule better than anyone else, and you can find some time to make this happen, not just for your partner but also for you.

Some women have time, but they don't feel sexy. Your sexuality is yours, my friend. It's up to you to feel sexy in your own skin. Take a long, hard look inside and figure out what would make you feel good about yourself. Stand in front of a mirror, naked and alone. Try to block out the opinions of others and pictures of airbrushed models. Instead of focusing on the things you aren't happy with, find some things that you are. Do you love your eyes and your hair? Maybe you really like your breasts or your booty. Focus on those things and play them up in the bedroom and out. Buy yourself some new lingerie, and don't just wear it to bed; wear it out to dinner or on your next date day. Hell, wear it to work. To be transparent, we are in our 40s. Our bodies are changing, and gravity is doing what it does best. We should own the changes that come with being in this decade. Aging is beautiful, and *eff* anyone who tells you differently.

CHAPTER 12

Cunningly shrewd
Physically attractive[16]

IF YOU'VE MADE IT THIS FAR, I'M BETTING YOU AREN'T offended by the title of this chapter.

Foxy is a state of mind, and we are going to talk about how to get there and how to own it.

Have you ever stood in front of the mirror naked and really looked at yourself objectively? I mentioned this in the previous chapter, but we are really going to dig in. What kind of thoughts went through your mind? Did you only see the things that you wish you could change, or did you acknowledge the things that you love about yourself? I will be completely honest. The first thing I see when I look in the mirror is my belly, and right behind it is my crepey skin. For years, I could only focus on the things that I saw as negative. I blame this on how our minds were inundated with images of super-thin models and airbrushed magazine pictures when we were young, and I'm not the only one. According to the Office on Women's Health, women are more likely to have a negative body image[17]. They cite

---

16 Merriam-Webster. (n.d.). Foxy. In *Merriam-Webster.com dictionary*. Retrieved August 23, 2024, from https://www.merriam-webster.com/dictionary/foxy

17 Office on Women's Health (2021, Feb. 17). Body Image. https://www.womenshealth.gov/mental-health/body-image-and-mental-health/body-image

many reasons for this, but one is that girls and women are more likely to be praised for their appearance than for their brainpower. We are also given standards of beauty that do not actually exist (back to airbrushing, etc.).

I've spent years trying to reframe the way that I see myself; change my lens, if you will. I still see those other things but when I realize that I am talking to myself in a way that I would hurt someone for talking to my daughters, I stop and make myself find three things that I love about my body. I'm going to put it on paper for you to read, and y'all, this is tough.

1. I love my booty. This has not always been true. For most of my adulthood, I suffered from noassatall disease. Y'all know what that is…no-ass-at-all. Here's the bonus to gaining 10 midlife pounds: I can see my booty, and I like the way it looks, with and without clothes. Cellulite and all!

2. I love my hair. It's a hot mess most days, but that matches my personality and my life so it's perfect for me. I've worn it short (pixie-style), medium, and long. It's been highlighted, colored, and natural; although, it's not been its natural color in years and probably won't be for a long time. It's wavy in some places and curly in others. It's different every day when I get up, but I get what I get, and I don't pitch a fit. It's 100% me.

3. I love the way I look from behind. I like my back. Since I've been doing more strength training, I like the way my waist looks, and I like the way the muscles flex; it reminds me that I am strong.

Just for fun, I asked Hubby what his three favorite things about my body were. First, I should explain that his love language is words of affection, so I was pretty sure that I knew what he would say. He was very quick to answer; it literally took milliseconds. He loves my booty ("because, dayum"), my belly ("because it's soft and sexy"), and my boobs ("since you've gained weight, they're bigger"). No surprises there. Then I asked him what his three favorite things were about his own body. He thought for a few seconds and said he wasn't sure. Ladies, we are not the only ones that struggle with this. Also, take note that one of his favorite parts of my body is not one of mine.

Let's change gears for a minute. Our confidence and self-worth should not be tied up in our appearance. Brains are sexy, too. Nothing makes me more frustrated than to see an intelligent woman, pretend to be less smart to try and "impress" someone. I'm sorry, but no. Just no. Your mind is where it's at, ladies! Smart is sexy, and you'll never convince me otherwise. Most of the time, brains outlast beauty, so own it, my friends. Let's try that mirror exercise again, and this time find three things you love about yourself that are not physical in nature. I'll go first, and to be totally honest, this was more difficult than deciding what I loved about my physical appearance:

1. I love how accepting I am of other people's differences. There have been times in my life when I felt this might be a fault, but it serves me well in my career and makes me easy to talk to (according to my patients).

2. I love how I am becoming more open to possibilities, and less closed off to change. We've already established how difficult change can be, but I am embracing it in this season of my life, and I'm happy with that.

3. I love that I am driven and competitive, but I am also laid back and even-tempered. I am goal-oriented and always have a plan for what comes next, which can drive Hubby crazy, but it keeps me on my toes. I also want to be good at everything I do, and I'm willing to work for it, but I'm not going to step on anyone else's toes to get there.

We owe it to ourselves and our fellow women in their 40s to speak empowerment and confidence to each other. As a nurse practitioner who works primarily in women's health, I try to leave every patient with a positive note. "I love your hair!". "You are smart, strong, and capable!". "Look at you, reaching goals and going after what you want!". There are enough people in the world trying to make life harder for us. We should not be doing it to each other.

We are often our worst critics, and we must let that go. Not only should we speak confidence to others, but we also need to speak it to ourselves. We will not feel foxy until we are able to love things about ourselves (bodies and minds). When I buy clothes, I look for things that make me feel confident (ask me about a snug red sweater dress I recently purchased that was way out of my comfort zone), but confidence doesn't start on the outside. It is only when we leave the opinions of others behind that we can fully define who we are. This is hard! Some days, I still struggle with this, but I will continue to fight, and when you see me out and about in a snug red dress, mind your business.

CHAPTER 13

Fulfilling

Providing happiness or satisfaction[18]

FULFILLMENT. WHAT DOES THAT WORD MEAN TO YOU? I'm at a point in my life where I am searching for it, but I realized that I wasn't really sure what that looked like for me. In this chapter, we are going to discuss different aspects of fulfillment, concentrating on professional, personal, and relationships, and yes, you can have one without the other.

Let's start with professional fulfillment. In some ways, I am qualified to speak to this, but in other ways, I am not. More on this later… In 2009, I finished a master's degree in nursing and obtained a family nurse practitioner certification. When I started that degree in 2007, I had an 8-month-old, a 3-year-old, a full-time job in nursing education, and Hubby and I were building a home. I was stressed to the max for that entire 2 years and, once finished, swore that I was done with school. "I'll never go back" were the words that I believe I said to Hubby after graduation. In 2018, I worked with a nurse practitioner student whom I had once taught in the dance studio. She was (and still is) super special to me, so when she tried to convince me to go back to school with her, I considered it. At first, I told her absolutely not, but y'all, I'm competitive. I could not imagine that I would be teaching

---

18 Merriam-Webster. (n.d.). Fulfilling. In *Merriam-Webster.com dictionary*. Retrieved August 23, 2024, from https://www.merriam-webster.com/dictionary/fulfilling

students in the clinic who would graduate with a higher degree than I had obtained. She (and Hubby) eventually talked me into it, and in 2019, I obtained a terminal degree in nursing (Thanks, Pish!). What does that even mean? I have a doctorate in nursing practice (DNP) degree. This means that I am considered an expert in reviewing research and evidence and applying it to nursing practice. A doctorate is the highest educational degree one can attain, and I once again told Hubby that "I'll never go back" after walking across that stage. He just smirked and said, "Whatever. We'll see.".

Educationally, I have attained the highest degree in my field. Professionally, I felt stuck. I had been working in public health since 2009 and often felt stagnant. I loved my job, and I adored my patients. Every day, I felt like we made a positive difference in someone's life. I have also been faculty in several nursing programs since 2005. I adore teaching and have so much love for students. Even so, I was not fulfilled professionally. I should have been, and I knew this, but I felt what I felt. I needed a new challenge. Enter this book idea. Many years ago, I did one of those fun social media quizzes where you ask your partner to answer a bunch of questions about you. One of the questions asked was, "If I ever become famous, what would it be for?". He thought for a minute and then said, "Writing a book." I think I probably laughed at him, but it planted a seed. I have been an avid reader my entire life (mostly of smutty romance books), but I never thought I would write anything like this.

In no way am I searching for fame, but maybe this is what I need to be professionally fulfilled. It's time for us to grab the bull by the horns. Life is short, and we need to seek out what makes us happy. We need to pay the bills, sure, but finding what challenges us and makes us feel satisfied is important. If you are there already, please share your accomplishments with the rest of us! If not, don't stop seeking that next opportunity. It might be what's been waiting for you all along.

Now for a more difficult discussion. Are you personally fulfilled? Can you honestly answer that question? When I first started writing this chapter, I couldn't. Well, I would have said yes, but I could not have told you why. The first step is answering the following question: What does personal fulfillment mean to me?". What are your life goals? Yours, not anyone else's. We've already discussed professional fulfillment, so let's leave that out. What do you want to accomplish in your personal life? Do you know? Have you ever taken time to really think about it? If not, now is the time! I found these things helpful when making my own list:

1. Try to cut down the weeds. Take a machete to those bastards if you must. Silence everyone else's expectations and desires and really think about what **YOU** want.

2. Write down your personal goals and put them somewhere you will see them frequently. I set a reminder on my phone. Every day at 7:00 am, my phone reminds me to "Die with memories, not dreams!". At 2:00 pm, it reminds me to "not listen to criticism from someone whom you would not seek advice." We are mothers, wives, sisters, and daughters. We have everyone else's needs and wants on our minds all the time. It's easy to forget about your goals if they aren't constantly in your face.

3. Celebrate the wins, even the small ones! If you get closer to attaining a personal goal, do something to mark the occasion. Girls' night? Date night? A bottle of your favorite wine? You choose! Just do *something* to commemorate the moment.

It's not easy to isolate what you really want and need. Figuring out what fulfills you is not for the inexperienced. We have lived and experienced a few things by this point in our lives, so it's a great time to give it some thought. What do you need, during the next decade, to make you feel satisfied personally? Go after that!

Finally, let's discuss relationships. Are you fulfilled in the important relationships in your life? One could argue that this is the same as personal fulfillment; however, I wholeheartedly believe that it is different. The reason personal fulfillment was discussed first is that you cannot be fulfilled in your relationships if you are not personally fulfilled on some level. Relationships involve a give-and-take environment, and you cannot pour out to others with an empty cup.

When you spend quality time with your partner, does just being together make you happy? If not, what would it take to get there? Marriage/partnerships take work. You cannot expect it to be easy. If you still have young children, or either of you are focused on your career, it can be difficult to carve out time to spend only with each other. Hear this: you should absolutely do it. Hubby and I have watched friends' marriages dissolve after the children are grown and gone, and we did not want that to happen to us. My dad taught us early in our relationship that continuing to date each other was important to maintaining a happy marriage. To continue to like each other, you must spend time and effort on each other.

What about your relationship with your children? Many of you still have young kids, and in some ways, I envy you. I miss the times when my girls wanted to spend most of their time with me. When they are young, first and foremost, you must be their parent. Teach them that they can trust you and that you always have their best interest at heart, even when it doesn't align with what they think they want. Be steadfast in your love for them; discipline them when it's needed; make time to attend their games or school events. Be present! Others of you, like me, have grown or nearly grown children. My oldest spread her wings and flew 10 hours away, and it was HARD! When she first moved, I made her text me several times a day and video call numerous times a week, just so I could ensure that she was okay. One of the hardest things I've ever done is learn how to parent an adult child! If you are here with me, now is the time to work on transitioning that relationship from one where you are in charge, to one where you are there for support. Become a friend, someone he/she can talk to about anything, and above all, someone they can trust. Finding fulfillment in a relationship with your children takes effort on your part. You are going to be the one that has to change as they get older. It's your job to figure out how to do that to cultivate a lasting relationship with your children.

Finding fulfillment in your life can be tough. It takes a little soul-searching to understand what you need to be fulfilled. Just in case you forgot, we are in our 40s, y'all. Believe it or not, it's time for us to start reaching this point! If you aren't there yet, it's not too late to start. Make this decade one to figure out what you need to be fulfilled. Find what fills your cup and make an effort to not let it get empty.

CHAPTER 14

Free

*Enjoying personal freedom: not subject to the control or domination of another
Having no obligations (as to work) or commitments
Not confined to a particular position or place; not united with, attached to, combined with, or mixed with something else[19]*

WOOHOO! WE MADE IT, AND I SAVED THE BEST FOR last. Free is by far my favorite F-word of my forties. Each year, I gain more personal freedom, feel less obligation to make commitments, and I am working toward no longer being confined to a particular place. I have more freedom now than ever before, and yes, it has some connection to my children growing up, but it is also a daily choice. I have learned to prioritize my time and effort, and I'm going to teach you how to make steps toward doing the same. In fact, this is what we've been working toward the entire book.

Are you overworked, overstimulated, and left with little to no time to yourself or for your family after you've worked 40(+) hours, cleaned the house, managed the kids, volunteered at church, baked 300 cookies for the PTO bake sale, and took the dog to the vet (and it's only Monday)? Friend, I've been there. In fact, I dare say that we all have. Not only do we feel pressured and obligated to sign our kids

---

[19] Merriam-Webster. (n.d.). Fulfilling. In *Merriam-Webster.com dictionary*. Retrieved August 23, 2024, from https://www.merriam-webster.com/dictionary/free

up for every type of activity known to man, but we also do the same for ourselves. Since when is it a sin for a woman to have a little free time? I was raised in church, and I know all about "idle hands" but let's be real. The faster you learn how to say no, the faster you are going to gain some control over your life.

If you are not one of us who struggle to say no then let me be the first to say, good for you! For the rest of us, let's review some of the reasons why we find this so difficult, I mean…it's only a two-letter word!

1. You may be a people pleaser. If this is your default, you may worry about what someone will think of you if you tell them no. You may also feel that it's easier to say yes than to risk the consequences of saying no.

2. You may have a guilt complex. This can be directly related to people pleasing, or it can be from other sources like childhood trauma, anxiety, culture (Hello, South…), or religion.

3. You may be an overachiever. Do you feel that you have to be Supermom? Are you a perfectionist? If so, you are not alone. We still live in a society where women have to fight for equal pay. For this reason alone, many fear the consequences of saying no.

If any of these describe you, it's time to get to work. There are lots of motivational podcasts and books to help you overcome these traits. Your time is precious, and you have to prioritize how you want to spend it. The next time someone asks you to volunteer or take on an additional task, spend a few minutes thinking about it before you respond. It's okay to tell them you need to check your calendar and get back to them. This will buy you some time to process. If you determine that it will bring you more stress than you can handle, just say no. You can pretty it up however you want, as long as you remember that "no" is your final answer.

Let's take a few minutes to think back about some of the chapter titles in this book. The first chapter was about fear. How does one gain freedom from fear? I believe it's by refusing to let fear rule your life. For example, I used to be afraid to fly but I really wanted to go places that only an airplane could take me. I had to face that fear head-on because I wanted to go more than I was afraid to fly. I think it also comes from time, experience, and just living life. We have enough years behind us now to know some things; quite a bit more than we did when we were younger. Let's use our knowledge and wisdom to help kick fear out of our lives.

We also need to seek freedom from toxic environments, be it family, friends, or work. Remember that you do not have to stay in a place or a relationship that is not good for you. You owe it to yourself to surround yourself with people who are supportive, honest, and uplifting. You are free to forgive and move forward with your life. Also, by this point in your career, you have likely worked hard and long enough to earn a place in an environment that appreciates all that you bring to the table. If not, it's time to start working toward that. In order to function at your highest level, you need to be in a supportive environment. If it's fear of failure that's keeping you in a toxic environment, remember that many times, we fail by not trying at all. Feel free to succeed (even if that means a little failure comes first). It is time for you to seek fulfillment; you've earned it!

The last (and my favorite) reminder is that you are free to feel good! It's time to get fit (mentally and physically), flaunt **your** fashion, be fierce, and remember that foxy is your middle name. If I had known that being forty came with all of these F-words, I would've been looking forward to it my whole life.